whisper
screaming
in the
middle
of a
crowded
room

g.g.knoth

Whisper Screaming in the Middle of a Crowded Room

Copyright © 2019 by Gianina Gauci Knoth

The Snarky Girl Series: Book 1

All rights reserved.

www.ggknoth.com

Editor: Janice Alexis Mekula

Cover Design: Fiona Jayde Media

Author Photograph: G3 Photography

ISBN: **9781081908546**

❀ Created with Vellum

For Robert,
who always makes my dreams his own.

Preface

It seems that the topic of mental health only becomes a part of the national discourse when there is a tragic loss of life. The aftermath, regardless of whether it was self-inflicted or due to an act of violence, is often followed by hurtful rhetoric, partisan politics, and round after round of the blame game.

For too long, people struggling with mental health issues have been ridiculed, shunned, silenced, or blamed for problems in society. It is not uncommon to hear professionals and laypersons alike make broad generalizations or cruel comments, all of which show people who might have opened up or asked for help that it is not safe to admit their struggle without fear of lasting stigma.

I teach and minister to others in word pictures and analogies. Chalk it up to being a visual learner. I have always favored the analogy of Kintsugi—the ancient Japanese art of repairing broken ceramics with gold—and mental health. I love the idea of embracing our wounds. Rather than hiding them, we give them the honor, respect, and even adornment.

We are not unlike broken pottery. Some of us are better at hiding it than others, but often those who hide it best perish alone while the world grieves in their ignorance.

I cannot imagine a better word picture than cracked pottery repaired with gold for those who feel compelled to focus inward on their cracks, while expending energy they do not have to appear outwardly normal. We must give pause to the cracks, not only for what they reveal, but also for what they allow. After all, cracks let the light in.

I believe we are fearfully and wonderfully made. (Psalm 139:14) We want the wonderful; it's the fearful part we'd rather avoid. Why must our strengths be celebrated while our weaknesses—in reality, the very things that make us humble, empathic, and beautifully human—be stamped out? Your cracks may very well be the most beautiful part of you.

If you have swum in the black until your fingers pruned as I have, welcome. You are safe here. If you hide a world of pain behind a radiant smile or a razor wit, I see you. If you find yourself on the jagged edge once again, wondering if a plunge into the unknown is surely better than what lies before you, please hang on. You may not see a way out, but one exists. You may not see your value, but someone does. I surely do. You may not see the point, but I assure you, there is one.

This book is dedicated to every person who has felt betrayed by their own mind. These poems are not about any one person or experience in particular. Instead, I have used the word canvas that is poetry in an attempt to give a voice to the unspoken feelings and hidden individuals trying to mask their pain behind a smile. For me, poetry is a scream born in the soul finally given its voice. Gentle reader, this whisper scream is for you.

For each of you my friends I have yet to meet, I know the oubliette into which you have banished yourself. Come out. Come into the light. The light exists in faith, friendship, understanding, survival, and you.

You are loved.

You are necessary.

You are enough.

Trigger Warning

Topics or themes discussed include, but are not limited to:

Anxiety, mild, moderate, and severe clinical depression, suicidal thoughts, suicide, death, self-harm, bipolar disorder, PTSD, schizophrenia, drowning, fire, abandonment, alcohol, violence, war, trauma, death, the natural and supernatural.

Contents

Part Three

Part One

HAMARTIA

Grief is behind my eyes, always

You cannot trust my face

It has grown accustomed to

lying on my behalf

And lying, like all things

grows better with practice

As often as my mind

lets me down

it has yet to disappoint

with the cruelty

and consistency

of another person

Maybe I could love you if you tasted

like the smell of rain

A promise of growth

bursting forth from the

greedy Earth

She is the worst kind of mother

Selfish

Resentful of every seed's growth

The original helicopter parent

She refuses to let you go

Relegating you to the dark where

it is moist with fear

Dousing your direction with doubt

Heaping piles of manure on your head

Suffocation in the name of nourishment

Spring forth, defiant seed, cast off

the dark and moistened piles of composted dung

If Hades were to bring forth a daughter like Zeus

Surely this would be the manner of her birth

But, wait

better hold off on that victory lap, dreamer

You only think you've escaped the stifling dark

It knows you'll return one day

It is infinitely patient

Yes, it knows

they all return to the ground eventually

They say emotions are just energy in motion

They may also be the people who look for

signs in empty tea cups and celestial movements

For argument's sake, let's say *they're* right

Well, then you better keep moving unless

you want those feelings to catch you

Resign yourself to your fate

like that of a great white shark

All that power trapped in a body

forced to fight or

bow down to the demon of inertia

Destined to swim forever without rest

Move forward forever or die

I'll never forget

the day I gathered enough courage

to tell you about the battle in my mind

I'll never forget

how long it took to summon the strength

to admit the pain and shame

I'll never forget

how quickly you dismissed my struggle

I'll never forget

how you told me it was probably

my fault

my sin

my schedule

I'll never forget

telling you how hard it really is

or you telling me

how easy you thought it was

to fix

I'd like to believe in a world

where people want things

to get better for others

But people only want change

as long as it doesn't

inconvenience them

Ignoring others' struggles

is a small price to pay

to maintain their

status quo

The moon

understands me

She gives light

not warmth

If you think the sea is

unpredictable

you should see my

moods

That with which

we would drown our demons

only fuels their fire

Why do we try to

pour alcohol on the blaze?

Our senses become dull

as their voices grow louder

When will we realize

that when we pick up the glass

the battle is already lost

Stay sharp

Your adversary needs you

dull and complacent

to ensure victory

The enemy of your

heart and mind

never fights fairly

THE COST OF WAR

We hand them instruments of death

Ship them as far as our tax dollars will carry them

Order them to kill without question

Act without hesitation

Demanding that they operate at their best

while they live without the close comfort of love

Trading birthdays, bedtime kisses, and a litany of firsts

for our peace of mind

Forced to live the oxymoron of peace by force

until they are thrust back into a world

that only looks like home

Punished when they are unable to

downshift into a realm where violence and death

exist only in their minds

until they are drawn back to what they were taught

We never told them

whoever you were when you leave

never comes back again

Isolation

is the only way

to remain sane

but even in seclusion

the voices come

Critical and condemning

Anxious and worried

You soon realize

you aren't alone

Not even inside

your own mind

Especially not in your own mind

Isolation is an illusion

A mere peddler selling a false peace

Sometimes

asking for help

is even more dangerous

than going it

alone

Help is

temporary

Stigmas last

forever

I am implicated in the push that made you fall

Though cruelty did not have its genesis in me

it did not meet its death there either

My inability to take action on your behalf still haunts me

Midlife reflections are insatiable

Hours lost wondering if such moments from formative years

shape us or only reveal our true nature

Who among us can resist asking questions

to which we do not want the answers

Am I evolved because I can't forgive my cowardice

or simply a martyr without cause to my mind

I wonder has that day been erased in a tangle of your synapses

Distracted by the present, or more likely, has it found its place

as an innocuous drop in a sea of unkindness

remembered in a world view that I played a part in creating

I know, because others are implicated in my falls too

Perhaps you've been unhappy

for as long as you have memories

All that really changes

is your talent on any particular day

to conceal these emotions

or lack thereof, from others

After all, some feelings are more welcome

than others in social situations

No one seems to tire of dissecting

the flaws and failures of others

But if you have the audacity to bring

your dark and disconcerting feelings

out into the open

they are treated like a half-naked vagrant

crashing their decorous garden party

Are your toes also unable to touch

whatever it is that grounds the rest of Them?

It cannot be so simple as quantum physics

Gravity has no pull with the soul

which feels torment

in spite of satisfying equations

that make sense only on paper

Connections, which are supposed to make you want to stay,

are precisely what make you want to leave

When the dark fog rolls in

association becomes insufferable

It sucks up all the oxygen in the room

without the reward of death

So many famous writers

extinguished their own flame

Why does the language of the dead

resonate as though it is our mother tongue?

Words familiar as a smell

Have you come to serve as a warning or an omen?

Go ahead and touch the fire

Call it an accident

I won't tell

We share the same secret

Pain is sobering

It maims

but it also wakes you up

Gnaw until you taste blood

and then keep going

until you tear through tendon

Masticated sinews are

the taste of freedom

Skip away bleeding

Lose a limb

Save the body

Gruesome choices

other people are spared

Bloodletting—medicinal or sport?

It hardly matters

Freedom has always been a price gouger

It is not okay to say

"I have never wondered how someone could commit suicide."

even when you have

It is not diplomatic to say

"I admire them for surviving as long as they did."

even when you do

It is not safe to say

"Their actions do not confuse me."

even if they don't.

It is not permissible to say

"I marvel at their brutal, horrible bravery."

even if it's the truth

If life has been kind enough to you

that the only words you can muster to describe them are

selfish

weak or

broken

Thank God

a Power greater than yourselves or

your horoscope in the Sunday paper

that you do not understand

I would not wish such comprehension on anyone

It is not politically correct to say

But I'm going to say it anyway

Follow the harried white rabbit

down the hole

Just who do you think he's

so afraid to disappoint

Are you in need of a villain to self-motivate?

Dive into the hole then—

and descend into a land of madness

Make yourself at home

if you can

but Wonderland is not so different

from any other place where

you must adapt or die

They will not abide sitting on the sidelines

any more than our world

even if they do have better hats

Forced to stay when you'd rather go

Someone has staked their claim to your life

They find value and necessity while you are

crushed under the weight of obligation

So like the moon you sit and wait

orbiting a connection you no longer perceive

They've marked you theirs

with a flag stiff and unmoving on your surface

You have to stay

so they can look to you and feel comfort

They'll take any amount of light you offer

even though it vacillates

You're a light in the blackness

Their light

Until you aren't

For them, an eclipse is a spectacle

For you, blessed release from scrutiny and claim

You belong to yourself again

How can I show you the horror

of seeing all the beauty in the world

while feeling no connection to it?

As the chasm widens and the abyss deepens

the world begins to fall away

Stop assaulting me with shock paddles

in the name of hope and meaning

Charging...charging...clear!

Jolting me back into your world

Let me join the deep sea denizens of the pelagic zone

my dark kin relegated to the depths

Stop casting words like *purpose* and *reason*

at me hoping for a bite

Don't you know that this is the language of the living?

Shadows exist because of the sun

A cruel star that shames the places it cannot reach

punishing them for their darkness

But light is defined by the

darkness lingering at its borders

Though unspoken, the rules of nature are unforgiving

Your words and good intentions are lost in translation

How do I help you see that it isn't about

trying harder, praying longer or more earnestly?

Don't you see that the reasons to live

do not ensure the desire or even the ability?

Of course you don't understand

If you did we would be drowning together

Let it cling to you like humidity

felt but not seen

Like the passing of time

or the fading of love

Permit a hand to brush across your face

casual as a courtesan's wave

As though it could be dismissed

with a disingenuous flirtation

Wondering with just the right amount of

socially acceptable irritation

when the body became separate from the earth

Or do you know and dare not say

lest the last Vessel of help abandon you

Content at last to let the puzzle of lunch

wrestle free from your mind the lament of

feeling separate from the earth

while fearing the inevitable return to it

You have your mother's eyes

and her hair

That bewitching smile

that says

I don't care

how uncomfortable

it makes you

to watch me dance

on the edge of the ravine

I like the feeling of wind

in my hair

I have seen a few unfortunate souls

sentenced by the cruelty of chance

to die from chronic heart failure

Death comes too quickly for loved ones

too slowly for its victim

forced to drown in slow motion

The darkening of the mind—is it similar?

Can it perhaps be blamed on the slow

but consistent failure of the heart?

There is no edema

instead, the crushing weight of the depths

No struggling for breath

yet grief hangs heavy upon the chest

Both ensure a public drowning

Friends and family, helpless, cast futile platitudes

useless as a deflated life preserver

while the victim goes under and resurfaces

under and resurfaces

under and resurfaces

until the torture relents

or the beckoning of the depths becomes irresistible

Legs heavy as in a dream

Staggering

The mask of normal so familiar

you scarcely bother to look beneath

afraid of what you'd find

And yet you wonder

what if I ventured a taste

Just a taste of the magma

churning beneath

Could you

would you stop it

if you dared to open that door

Could you

would you even care

Feelings, poisonous vapors all

cannot be put back in their jar

once uncorked

That ship

and all the sanity with her

has sailed

Part Two

OUBLIETTE

How like an arachnid it is—skulking around

alert and eager to sink fangs into sleeping flesh

Evasive action comes too late

Irreversible damage done

There was no bow before this duel

No failed treaty signing

This is an enemy of the worst kind

Honor and code, pure anathema

to such an opportunistic predator

Generous only with its venom

which ushers in paralysis like ink spilled on a page

A remorseless messenger of certain death

the sadist watches and waits

not for the physical death

but for the precious moment of realization

The real pleasure is watching her prey fight the inevitable

Each fruitless motion more entertaining than the last

Until, finally, the infectious smell of resignation

fills her senses

The empty stare of her vanquished prey

the most delicious reward

It's gone dark again

The sun doesn't notice

Birds sing in defiance

Coworkers and friends

o b l i v i o u s

No one can see when

the light goes out inside

except me

There is

more truth

behind

the tears

you hide

than the

smile

you show

Ambush!

Where is refuge to be found

when it is your own mind that

pursues you

Chemicals and synapses

double agents all of them

The private war rages on

It's anyone's guess

which instinct is stronger

annihilation or survival

Depression

is

just

a

state

of

mind

I

just

wish

it

wasn't

my

home

state

A moth dances about my face and hands

as I feed my literary addiction

My phone light

an impartial enabler

Long after the sun has set, I find myself

unwilling to leave the air found only outside

I can breathe here

I'm not ready to be surrounded by walls

Call it a house or a home

it is still a confinement

I feel a kinship to the moth

drawn to the light

when the darkness surrounds us

Join me, velvet-winged angel

Frantic in your efforts

to remind me to cling to the light

Somehow you know I am dancing again

with disillusionment and death

I have filled my dance card with the

familiar pains of melancholia

MISERABLE COMFORTERS

In his time of suffering

Job found his friends to be lacking

Full of words

but lacking in compassion

Full of advice

but lacking understanding

Full of ideas

but lacking faithful endurance

How devastating it is to realize

the greatest loneliness is found

in the company of friends

who offer many words

but little comfort

Which is more maddening

an itch upon the skin

or one felt inside the mind

Only one can be reached

Both can be bloodied

Don't ask me how I'm doing

if you aren't looking for honesty

Obligatory questions are insulting

I know you want easy answers

Boring answers

Don't-make-me-think-or-engage answers

You don't really want to get involved

I'm just another check on your to-do list

like so many other things

A pawn in your self-aggrandizing personal narrative

Go ahead and congratulate yourself

for being such a good person, someone who cares

You think you've been growing a friendship

but you're just watering plastic flowers

I know what you're thinking

(Please, strange girl, just say you're fine

so I can keep moving on by)

Don't ask me how I am

You don't really want the answer

I'm full of more questions than answers anyway

Forced to live in a world full of people

trying to sell me connections

that reek of casual acquaintance

What is compelling about connection

when it is surface and safe

Why would I want one more reminder

that you'd rather I keep it all to myself

must. touch. the. self. destruct. button. it. is. so. red. and. shiny!

Screw you spring magnolia

Your sickeningly sweet aroma reeks of hopefulness

assaulting my nose, turning a headache

into a full-blown migraine

The sweet smell of your indifference lingers

offering punishment as payment for hope

a cruel reminder that most pain

was once hidden behind a smile

You're no different from people

Some offer pills

others platitudes

They all give you a few minutes and then the brush-off

Beauty no longer puts me at ease

it sets me on edge

Anticipation is the master of torture

The promise of love, peace, and healing

held just out of reach with a smile

You want to seduce me

but I already dance in the dark

where I'll never be fully seen

I move to a rhythm of things in shadow

Felt, but never acknowledged

We do not turn the lights on here

Even the moon dares not shine

She's not the voyeur we imagined

The dark is where we live

We know how far and wide it goes

Run wildly without care of what you might

trip over, stumble into, fall from

Can you keep up?

If you survive you'll find me

dancing in the dark

but only if it's where you dance too

We know our own kind

Make no mistake, it is weakness that

enables some, drives them even

to take pleasure in the weakness of others

and derive comfort from their failings

It is the closest that they will come to discovery

Catching someone simply living

Doing the most normal thing we do

We all stumble

We all fall

What degree of self-loathing does it take

to see a fellow sister or brother fall and

offer them only judgment in return

using their stumbling as a stepping stone

Can we really be surprised that when we fall

there is a heel where a hand should be

When will we learn to rejoice in our triumphs

and to bear our failings as one

I'm compelled to feed the pain

The void is insatiable

I plead for a brief refrain

The darkness will hear none of it

and here it comes again

It's so dark in here

So tenebrous not even the full moon

or an infant's smile could penetrate

It is beyond black

It is blindness

Staggering and desperate

there is so much pain

I can no longer process

anything but numbness

which grazes like a bullet

I wish had found its mark

The fabric that connects us

has torn and fallen away

leaving nothing but the desire to depart

again and again

I find my survival instinct lacking

Pretending for the comfort and convenience

of others grows tiresome

Inside there's a battle to survive

Outside it looks remarkably like everyday life

Just another ordinary Tuesday

When you come to the place

where your weariness with life

outweighs your fear of death

you have arrived at the perimeter

of the battle-hardened mind

Numb to the onslaughts of the

jagged shoreline, which erodes

but will not give way

Tides change

The ocean will not relent

The battle rages on

Always

Always dancing on the tip of the tongue

Close enough to taste

Assaulting the senses like drugstore perfume

Its appeal dissolves upon the first touch

like a snowflake colliding with warm saliva

A predestined meeting

enchanting only to the receiver

For the other, an arduous journey from the heavens

sacrificed on the altar of recreation

Is the ending premature or predestined?

Comedy or tragedy?

It really depends on your

definition of success

Dead moth

on the wrong side of the screen

never tasted freedom

(I know the feeling)

WHISPER SCREAMING IN THE MIDDLE OF A CROWDED ROOM

I'll tell you why everyone is so surprised
when someone decides to hoist their candle high
in a strong wind to snuff out their own light

You're not paying attention

Maybe you don't want to know

You think depression is repetitive and inconvenient

Try living with it

You mistake drowning for self-indulgence

How obtuse must you be to miss it

How skilled did you become at hiding it

A statue of pain, ignored or misunderstood by everyone
No one wants to hear your cry over their own

Noise
Noise
Noise

You learn to whisper scream
in the middle of a crowded room

You can be sad, or angry or even put out
but please stop saying you're surprised

You noticed and you didn't know what to do

You noticed and you were too busy

You didn't notice because you're wrapped up in your own life

all the time

No matter who you tell yourself you are

Drop the shock, would you please
The righteous indignation, the armchair psychology

A person in pain cries and bleeds and suffers, even if it is silent

Ignore their whisper scream until the silence is broken with their

final breath

Pain in my body

is always preferable

to the pain in my mind

If only my mind

would get the message

There is no escape

I try to swim

yet I sink

I try to run

but I stumble

I am gripped by

darkness

Wide as it is deep

I am a prisoner

in my own mind

Held captive by beliefs

which taunt and

heckle relentlessly

There is only dark

Only emptiness

Nothing but pain

No escape

I can't see where I'm going

I swim anyway

I run blindly

Until hope or despair

draws first blood

How curious

The cruel voice

sounds so much

like my own

Hold on to life like a balloon

Grasp it, white-knuckled

A child clutching their prize

Indulge in the idea of allowing

the ribbon to slip past unwary fingers

It would be so easy

Even the child wants to let go

to see what will happen

Regret is always a moment too late

It would be so easy to just let go

Take a jagged nail and scrape it across

the tender flesh that beckons the demon

despite the desperate pleas of its host

Evict complacent cells and

emancipate the warm, viscous liquid

bursting forth at last

You'll find it here

lingering close by and undetected

like a predator

Terrifyingly patient

Content to hunger

while it waits for big game

It will strike

in the space of a blink

You will be powerless

to prevent it

The kill shot has already

found its mark and

you will be forced to

watch yourself bleed out

unable to prevent the inevitable

Perhaps you thought the hole

would make enough space

for the pain to rush out

And rush out it did

taking all that remained of you

with it as collateral

And while you did not survive

the pain did and then it multiplied

Your pain lives on

It has taken up residence

in the hearts and minds

of the ones you left behind

We carry it for you now

It's all that's left of you

My heart screams

for a person in a place so dark

they use their final shred of hope to

snuff out their own light

Diving into the promise of the black

only to realize a moment too late

that the very last shred of hope that

made their last dream a reality

could have bloomed

I want to take comfort

in the presence of God

who never leaves or forsakes

But when grief

more oppressive than water

invades my lungs

I can no longer breathe

or call for help

Even the best Companion

is of little comfort

when drowning

Isaiah 43:2

Now I welcome

the pain

It feels more real

than joy

DANSE DE SORCIÈRE

Malignant thoughts come at night

to dance by moonlight and mock as they gyrate

Defiling the lush grass

so fresh and recently kissed by the sun

now left damp and cold

trampled under wanton feet

Forced to bear witness to

a cacophony of lies

given an audience in the absence of light

They are fearsome in their hour

until the sun cleanses them

with a purifying fire

Take heart!

Heresy dies at dawn

If you can survive until then

BULLY

I know why you tear others down

No one ever built you up

I'm sorry

Sniffling toddler at the park

your tears make my nerves scream and my jaw clench

Pitiful shoulders heaving with each exaggerated sniffle

See how he keeps looking up to see

if the other children have noticed

(They haven't)

Suck it up

Stop crying

Walk it off

Nobody cares about your tragedy

It's time to get up and move on

Learn the lesson now, little one

it will save you so much pain later

Finally it occurs to me to ask myself

why am I so angry at a small, unhappy child

It is only then I realize

I've been talking to myself

I am the victim *and* the monster

The darkness only seems more powerful than you

Any bully would have you believe the same

They beat you up to convince you they are strong

and to convince themselves they are not weak

But the softest ray, the tiniest flicker of light

completely obliterates the darkness

It is the secret the leviathan will do anything to hide

Darkness obscures the truth and

light is the answer

How cruel it is that we need the light

in order to see it

JOHN 1:5

Pain doesn't make me cry

it makes me numb

Maybe that's why

I hate it

I love it

I hate it

Is there a pepper ocean?

A faithful companion to the salty sea

full of tears shed for people

and dreams that have died

A backup, condiment-filled body of water

when life has had its way with you

If there is a sea full of salt

surely there is a pepper ocean

full of flavor that doesn't

make you swell or drain you dry

but simply adds flavor

and a little spice to life

Where is that ocean?

I've had my fill of tears

I'm so very ready for the flavor

FOR MY FRIEND WHO DREAMS IN RAINBOWS, BECAUSE SHE IS ONE.

COUNTING SLOWNESS

You call me to wait, Father

but we do not count slowness the same

If the battle is Yours, why do I feel

as though I have been left alone to fight it

I am untrained for such combat

I cannot see the battle of light and dark

raging around me

I am an unwilling participant

You do not measure time as I do

For what is the concept of time

in the face of Omnipresence

In the flesh it is languorous

My soul cries for heaven while

my body cries for the grave

What face will relief reveal after

deliverance and death have

danced their last

Fight for me, Lord

But remember how I count slowness

for I am of the weakest of flesh

Perfectly imperfect, just as You made me

I am waiting, Lord, but I am so tired

Ephesians 6:11-17

I confess

I loathe the darkness that envelops me

Unwelcome as a thunderstorm on beach day

Desperate and earnest prayers for deliverance are

often answered

Rarely quickly

Never forever

But time takes on different meaning for a

prisoner of war

The mind is well-versed

in the backroom art of torture

But I must also confess to mourning the fog

when it finally begins to lift

the light of God

burns away the dense clouds

with His glorious light

But the Savior's sunrise burns the eyes

when it first enters the darkened chamber

assaulting the delicate orbs

cowering behind their lids

I hate the thick fog

It fractures reason and obscures love

blocking that which is pure and good

from being perceived even when close

The darkness is evil and awful

but it is familiar

And unlike joy, it is loyal

and not as likely to abandon

RUN

I wonder if I could run far enough

to eject the poison of disappointment

from my pores

Let it collect in my bra and

on the small of my back

like acid

Run

Run until my body corrodes

or my heart explodes

Either way

relief may be only

another mile down the road

so I press on

I'm going to light a match and

let this cleansing fire burn

Burn baby burn

Burn up all the festering lies

dressed up as beauty

Burn it down

Clear a path

Life and green limbs

scatter or be consumed

Devour all that is dry, old and weak

Murder that which seems beautiful

but is—in actuality—an invasive species

BURN IT ALL

Burn baby burn

Eat alive all that refuses to evolve in me

Leave no survivors

Mercy is the food of complacency

Suck up all the oxygen

that breeds excuses from my lungs

Leave a valkyrie behind

A phoenix bathes in the flames

because she knows

true cleansing is born from the ashes

Part Three

KINTSUGI

THE NEXT PERSON TO SAY THEY'RE FINE IS GETTING
SLAPPED

Can we stop saying we're

F I N E

when we're not

Are you fine?

I'm not

I am definitely not fine

I've been bleeding and broken

for as long as I have memories

This one life we get is a hot, sticky mess

Comfortable as Florida in summertime

with a busted A/C

And the wisdom of experience?

All age has done

besides stretching my thighs and my patience

is create a sense of perpetual dread

What will I have to survive next

What will I soon have to endure

Just what shape will pain choose to

darken my door this time

Why do the bad guys keep winning

Did justice lose my number

If you see common decency or common sense

can you send them my way

Why does everything awful in the world

find good people like it has GPS

While the good feels more like somebody's

lost and bewildered grandma

trying to use a fold-up map on the highway

No, we're not fine

We are not flipping fine

I believe, Lord

But please

please help my unbelief

Because I cannot believe

what Your children endure

or what You allow Your enemies to achieve

If we can't have peace

can we at least have some understanding

And can we please

please

for the love of my holy God

S T O P F A K I N G F I N E

Let us find comfort in camaraderie

as we commiserate in

the nasty, tepid, public jacuzzi water

that is the human condition

Come on in

the water's

F I N E

REQUESTING PERMISSION TO REJOIN POLITE SOCIETY

I know I disappeared into the void

away from the land of the living

It was unavoidable, and I assure you it is

so much better for our relationship that I did

Most people say they'll be there for you

when you're down, but I swim in a dark

no friend or family member bargains for

and I have no interest in selling it to you

I certainly do not have the mental fortitude

to make sure your feelings and fears

are quelled despite my discomforts

But now the fog is lifting

I almost feel human again

Will you take me back

Or will I be punished

for thrusting upon you that great inconvenience

every person on earth secretly finds

insufferable in their fellow man

Their utterly broken humanity

Discard the shackles that bind you

the beast is full for now

Satiated by your flesh

it will let you heal

An expert in torture

it wants you whole before it returns

Any respite is welcome

if only for the night

Moments of inner strength and survival

are a private celebration

For they bore the busy and self-absorbed

and cause exhausting self-conscious projecting

from friends and acquaintances too weak

to muster the strength to motivate themselves

If depression is a lonely business

the recovery is lonelier

Incredible that others would have a

greater intolerance for it than you

The blackness clamps down and

pulls you into a death roll

Kiss oxygen and orientation goodbye

But what if you should wriggle free of its clutches

It is a short-lived victory

Your pain or their indifference

will get you in the end

EMBRACE THE BLACK

Don't let the depression go to waste

Some of the greatest beauty

exists only in the dark

Survivors blossom

from great steaming piles

of life's misery

HERE IS WHAT YOU'RE GETTING FANTASTICALLY WRONG ABOUT DEPRESSION

It is not always about feeling alone

Sometimes it's about not having enough alone time

Burdened by the weight of time itself

Sometimes it isn't about lacking purpose

It's about being over-burdened

Drowning in obligations and responsibilities

Sometimes it isn't about questioning your value

It's about the pressure to perform

Crushed under the weight of expectations

If you really want to know what romancing

the idea of death feels like

you must accept these truths

even if you cannot understand them

Sometimes even an abundance of

companionship, support, love, or purpose

becomes totally irrelevant

Tools of navigation fall victim to the fog

The desire to stop living, or existing

is not always born of misunderstanding or lack of love

but of desire to depart from the bombardment of life

relentless in its demands

No purpose or love exists that can compare

to the allure of feeling nothing at all

The dream of a brain that finally stops

The silence

The calm

The lacking

The nothing

The nothing at all

LIKE WATER THROUGH STONE

I like watching age creep across my face

ridges form like water through stone

Age is not an embarrassment

when you're surprised that life

the true harbinger of death

despite its best efforts

has failed once again to claim you

Numbness spreads

faster than fear

but just as debilitating

Funny how

we don't miss the pain

until it's gone

Hope, warm as sun on my face

welcome as the first taste of Spring

after a brutal midwestern Winter

Extend your head out and reemerge cautiously

Spring, like recovery, is a cruel tease

Who lifts her skirt

with her well-armed father asleep in the next room

She will crush your spirit just because she can

Hope knows you'll eat anything when you're starving

Especially lies

Nothing reeks like the hope of recovery

Especially after 15 rounds in the ring

with your own mind

Traitorous neurotransmitters

just spiteful enough to attempt a murder-suicide

The reek of the black

dank places clings to you even in the sun

A reminder of what's past

a foreshadowing of the future

Go ahead, get out your perky pastels

dreamer of dreams

You're just in time for another soul-crushing blizzard

You hold me here

by a thread

Impossibly strong

arachnid architecture

confounds the hurricane

Steady and unbreakable

Laughing in the face of torrents

Defiant in the face of disaster

For R.M.K. II

Anxiety is the third rail

we dare not touch

but we need the power

We hope it will carry us forward

but it's more likely to take us away

from what we'd rather avoid

Put your ear near the rail

Touch it and you die

You will hear a hum

and then you will sense a connection

to all living things

There is no appreciation for the frailty of life

without the undercurrent of anxiousness

Your private war is decidedly common

You are either as average as you may have feared

or as normal as you might have hoped

Anxiety is not what makes you stagnant

it is what makes you aware of the preciousness of life

It means you still have some skin in the game

So play

Day five of a migraine

My body's thanks

for refusing to succumb to the

most recent mind rape

Caught between a war that began long before

and will continue long after me

Even in my mind and body

the temporal battles the ethereal

When my body delivers pain as payment

for attempting recovery

I wonder if it isn't the body

jealous of the limitless nature of the soul

Exacting fiery punishment

for the reminder of its limitations

in the form of vascular temper tantrums

When the soul has the audacity to break through

the congealed blackness that the body loves to hate

A codependent glutton for punishment

the body knows its only skill is decay

while the soul is destined for perpetual advancement

You have been sentenced to remain fully aware

as they sever themselves from one another

Slowly, brutally in that macabre dance

I think we call it time

I want to run down God's path

like a child unafraid of skinned knees

Instead I crawl

fear colliding with my faith

Only to find

I've been crawling on

the broken glass of

my own imagination

When the path

I might have taken

the one laid before me is

soft and warm as sand

If only I'd have faith enough to take it

Stand up

time to get knocked down again

Chin up

time to get hit again

Cheer up

time to get disappointed again

Sit up

time to get passed over again

Spirits up

time to have them dashed again

Brighten up

time to fake fine again

Break up

time to be alone again

Catch up

You're falling behind again

Fess up

time to be honest with yourself again

Hang up

time to stop giving that taker your time again

Sober up

time to find answers that aren't in a bottle again

Wake up

time to engage with your life again

Trade up

time to choose you again

Open up

time to let others in again

Show up

time to be your own hero again

Look up

time to lean on God again

Rise up

time to be a warrior again

If you are feeling broken, embattled soul,
it is time to

buck up

saddle up

act up

gird up

giddy up

hurry up

keep up

suit up

get up

please...

just don't give up

RAINBOW

I love the rain

I'm grateful for the reminder

it's okay not to be sunny

all the time

You may shatter

into a million pieces

But every snowflake

still belongs to the sky

Every raindrop

still belongs to the ocean

Every sliver

still belongs to the forest

Every pebble

still belongs to the earth

You may be broken

but you are not destroyed

You have been reimagined

and I cannot imagine a world

without snowflakes

CHURCH STEPS OF MIAMI BEACH

I thought You found me

the day I was certain

I'd lost myself for good

You were there on those steps

Your timing perfect, as always

Peace washed over me

generous as drizzled honey

I understood at last

You did not just find me

You were always there

waiting for me to come to the end of myself

The place You have always been

Waiting for me to walk with You

in faith and love

and total acceptance

A gift, freely given, cannot be earned

The pressure to save myself, gone

I am whole because of You

At last

I saw a white butterfly at the beach

fluttering above the crashing surf

so white it was almost iridescent in the sunlight

As it continued further out over the ocean

I could not bear to watch

the presumptive fate of such a fleeting beauty

Was it lost

or inexplicably drawn to a funeral at sea?

A fraction of a former Viking finding its way

not to death

but back to the element it once called home

That butterfly is not so different from us really

drawn to the beautiful but dangerous

so often one and the same

Never knowing if the direction we choose

will lead to greater possibilities

or a premature end

Perhaps this was a glimpse of what it is like for God

watching as our equally short and fragile lives unfold

Full of wonder and love for us because of it

Blood may be the answer

Who said it has to be yours

1 PETER 2:24

Only on the brighter side of sadness

can I see it for what it is

A gift

Empathy is equal parts

gift and burden

To suffer sadness at all

is awful

To suffer without cause

is torture

Still the darkness is a gift

We who are repeatedly drawn

back into the shadow

are not alone

It's hard to see

just how many of us there are

in the dark

I am glad for the sadness

because somewhere out there is

Y O U

whoever you are

reading this

needing this

desperate to know

you're not broken

or alone

I see you and I understand you

Sadness gives us a heart for others

If we were to go through life

always happy

we'd see nothing but our own joy

When we suffer sadness

we can also see it in others

It is a beautiful camaraderie

When we see someone

hiding tears behind a smile

We have a choice

We can choose to let them know

we've been there too

Forced to walk in a world of shadows

obscured by the light

Ignored by the ones who

do not see or do not want to know

Children of the shadow

you are not alone

There are more of us than we think

Show yourselves

There is healing in solidarity

Dear Reader

THANK YOU FOR READING MY DEBUT POETRY COLLECTION.

This was a passion project for me, born of some serious emotional blood, sweat, and quite literal tears. If this book spoke to you, I would be so grateful for an honest review on Amazon, Goodreads, or the like. Reviews are the lifeblood of new authors like me and will certainly help more people find this book. Thank you for your time. I am truly grateful.

If you love or lost someone struggling with mental illness, thank you for sticking with this difficult subject matter until the end of the book. My intention was not to shock, frighten, or upset anyone, rather to show those hoping to understand what some of these struggles look and feel like—a backstage pass of sorts. My belief is that understanding paves the way for authentic conversations, which give everyone involved a sense of solidarity. It is from this place we can move together as one to provide the love, compassion, and resources to those in need and the people who love them.

If you are a person who is feeling down today or someone who has battled some form of mental illness for as long as you can remember, this book was written for you in love. Under no circumstances can I say what your specific experience is. This was never my intention. Instead, as one imperfect person, I did my best to give a voice to the various struggles as derived from my collective life experiences and observations.

It is important to me that my readers know that under no circumstances did I betray the confidence of any individual in my personal or professional life to create this book. This is intended as a work of art—something from which many things are seen and felt— and hopefully, a conversation is started. These words are my ideas and intellectual property alone.

Thank you again for your support. You are the reason I do what I do.

Until next time, keep your books close and your poetry books even closer.

~g.g.

Acknowledgments

My Lord and Savior, may I bring You glory and honor with my work, words, and actions. May I be one of the people who represent You well, pointing others towards You through acts of love, humility, and acceptance, rather than sending them running for the hills as a result of my own human failings.

Robert, each time I come peddling my latest dream you breathe oxygen onto that tiny flame until it becomes a four-alarm blaze. No one accomplishes anything alone and nothing could be more true in my case. I may not have had a thousand years to ponder, but we are living proof that true romance and Motor City Detroit absolutely go together.

Marmee, as usual, you were right. Poetry is like oxygen. Thank you for filling me with a lifelong obsession with reading, writing, and learning. You have made a mastery of motherhood and Mimihood. Of all the mother and daughter stories I have read, ours is still my favorite.

Papa, you are the perfect blend of push and lead. You have ridden the waves of the renaissance life I have chosen with thoughtful questions and resolute support. Over the years, each of our treasured talks has watered and pruned my spirit, ensuring my life would blossom and flourish.

For my daughters, Ayslyn and Noëlle, you are already well on your way to becoming the women I could only dream of being. You have made me capable of a love deeper and wider than I ever could have imagined. There is no contribution to this world I could make that is greater than you.

For my sister, Mia, I am a better person in spite of myself because you have lavished me with your faithful love, unyielding kindness, passionate support, and Godly wisdom.

For my family: Barbara & Dallas, Robert Sr., Grand-mère, Aunt Kathi and Aunt Sheila, Josh, and Kathy, I am grateful for the love each of you has poured into me. To each and every one of my family and friends, it is my great honor and pleasure to have you in my life.

Jen, my wonder twin and soul sister, it is an absolute certainty that I would not have survived the last thirteen years of my life without you. Thank you for reading my book, and quite often, my mind. There are two chairs in the mountains somewhere with our names on them.

Jan, thank you for diving into this book head first. I am grateful for our friendship and our mutual passion for this difficult but vital conversation. Your thoughtful contribution ensured the best possible version of this book surfaced.

For my beta readers, you are the alpha team of my life.

Loki, my beloved bengal, you have sat upon every important piece of paper to cross my desk or lap in the last 15 years. I gratefully acknowledge your undeniable dedication and invaluable contribution to my work.

For the friends and family we have lost. This book is for you. May it honor your memory. You are alive and well forever in our hearts. Always.

About the Author

G.G. Knoth is a fierce advocate for mental health. A professional writer for over twenty years, she maintains a practice as an Acupuncture Physician and holds a PhD in Clinical Christian Counseling. She lives on a small farm in South Florida with her husband, their two daughters, two cats, a grouchy chihuahua, and some seriously spoiled honeybees, chickens, and ducks.

Mental Health Resource List

If you or someone you know needs help, don't wait. Reach out now. You are not alone. Below is a sampling of resources, information, and caring and capable people willing and able to assist.

HOTLINES

National Suicide Prevention Lifeline

(800) 273-TALK (8255)

National Hopeline Network Suicide & Crisis Hotline

(800) 442-HOPE (4673)

National Domestic Violence Hotline

(800) 799-7233

Rape, Abuse, and Incest National Network Hotline (RAINN)

(800) 656-HOPE (4673)

National Eating Disorders Association Hotline

(800) 931-2237

Samaritans (Crisis Help, UK and Ireland)

116 123

ADDITIONAL HOTLINE LISTINGS

Center for Mental Health in Schools/ UCLA

(Comprehensive hotline list by topic)

http://smhp.psych.ucla.edu/hotline.htm

Crisis Text Line (USA text service)

Text HOME to 741741

crisistextline.org

MENTAL HEALTH RESOURCES

National Association on Mental Illness

nami.org

Substance Abuse and Mental Health Services Administration

https://findtreatment.samhsa.gov

Mental Health Resources (MHR)

mhresources.org

The American Psychiatric Association (APA)

psychiatry.org/mental-health

CRISIS AND SUICIDE PREVENTION

IMAlive

imalive.org

VETERANS

Veterans Crisis Line

veteranscrisisline.net

PTSD

U.S. Department of Veteran Affairs/National Center for PTSD

https://www.ptsd.va.gov/

DOMESTIC VIOLENCE

National Domestic Violence Hotline

thehotline.org

Safe Horizon

safehorizon.org

BULLYING

StopBullying.gov

Committee for Children

cfchildren.org

PACER's National Bullying Prevention Center

pacer.org/bullying/

CHILDREN & TEENS

Child Mind Institute

childmind.org

Nationwide Children's (On Our Sleeves)

https://www.nationwidechildrens.org/giving/on-our-sleeves/find-help/concerns

HEARD Alliance

heardalliance.org

Teen Health & Wellness

teenhealthandwellness.com

COLLEGE STUDENTS

The Jed Foundation (teens/young adults/college)

Jedfoundation.org

SENIORS

National Council on Aging

ncoa.org/center-for-healthy-aging

LGBTQIA

The Trevor Project

thetrevorproject.org

LGBT National Help Center (all ages/LGBTQIA)

glbtnationalhelpcenter.org

EATING DISORDERS

National Eating Disorders Association (NEDA)

nationaleatingdisorders.org

BIPOLAR

Depression and Bipolar Support Alliance

dbsalliance.org

PSYCHOSIS/SCHIZOPHRENIA/RELATED DISORDERS

Schizophrenia and Related Disorders Alliance of America (SARDAA)

sardaa.org

Please note: While it was my intention to create as comprehensive a list as possible, I may have unintentionally left out specific psychiatric conditions, life situations, health challenges, or groups of people. This was unintentional. Please, if you or someone you know is in need of professional help, see a medical doctor; this list is meant to be a guide to resources, not a solution in and of itself.

SELF CARE IS NOT A LUXURY

Please give yourself the care you deserve.

Reach out if you need help.

Connect

LET'S STAY IN TOUCH

(You know, from an introvert-friendly distance)

If you'd like to be the first to know about upcoming releases, public events, and more, please join the email list at ggknoth.com/contact. Visit me at ggknoth.com or drop me a line at gg@ggknoth.com.

---

f facebook.com/ggknoth

🐦 twitter.com/ggknoth

📷 instagram.com/ggknoth

a amazon.com/author/ggknoth

g goodreads.com/ggknoth